CATECHISM OF

ST. GERTRUDE

THE GREAT

Revealing the Love and Mercy of Jesus Christ to Souls...

(Excerpts from <u>The Life and Revelations of St. Gertrude the Great</u>)

There was once a time in the Middle Ages considered to be the Golden Age of the Mystics--the 13th century was an eventful one for the world and the Church. At its beginning, the founding of the great Orders of the Church-St. Dominic and St. Francis established in almost every city of Europe; hundreds, maybe thousands of saints and martyrs already gone to their heavenly reward. St. Elizabeth of Hungary had sanctified a peace and edified a nation by her heroic virtue and meek resignation in adversity. St. Thomas Aquinas and the seraphic St. Bonaventure had bequeathed such treasures to the Church as had never been confided to her keeping. St. Louis had died a victim to his love of Jesus Crucified and his grief that the land where his Lord had died should be despoiled by the heathens and infidels.

It was a century of saints and of saints or extraordinary note; at the close of this century, as a crowning gift, came the great and beautiful St. Gertrude, whose history has been too little known among us, while her very name receives a continual homage of reverent love.

Gertrude was born at Eiselben, a small town in the county of Mansfield, on the 6th of January,1263. When the Saint reached her 5th year, she was placed in the famous Benedictine Abbey of Rodersdorf, in the diocese of Halberstadt, where she was soon joined by her younger sister, Mechtilde.

Here, under the careful training of the Benedictine nuns; who then, as now, devoted themselves with unwearied solicitude, and more than ordinary intellectual abilities, to the education of those confided to their charge—the young Countess of Lachenborn advanced in wisdom and learning, both human and divine.

The Saint has informed us herself when and how the first of these heavenly communications was given to her. It was on Monday, January 25th "at the close of day, the Light of lights came to dissipate the obscurity of her darkness, and to commence her conversion."

And Jesus came, as He mostly comes to His beloved ones, as she performed an act of humility and obedience—declining to an ancient religious to fulfill a conventual observance, and doubtless from no mere habitual custom, but with deep and lowly reverence for a spouse of Christ, whom she considered incomparably her superior in virtue and sanctity.

A person whose sanctity had been long manifest, and who was specially favored by Divine communications, came to the monastery from a distant country to obtain an interview with the Saint. As she knew none of the religious personally, she prayed that whoever would benefit her soul most by their conversation might be sent to her. It was then made known to her that whoever should come and take their place beside her would be indeed the one most beloved by God, and the most holy among the religious.

On her arrival, St. Gertrude came to her; but so well did she conceal any appearance of sanctity and hide the supernatural light with which she was favored, that the stranger imagined she had been deceived and again prayed as she had done before. The same reply was once more given to her and she was assured that this was indeed the religious who was so dear to God.

Shortly after, the visitor had a long interview with St. Mechtilde whose conversation she greatly preferred, and whose sanctity was more apparent. Again, she "inquired of God," and asked why St. Gertrude was preferred to her sister. Our Lord replied that He had indeed operated great graces in Mechtilde, but in Gertrude He had operated, and He would yet operate, far greater.

Another person of great sanctity who was praying for the Saint, felt a singular impulse of affection for her, which she believed to be supernatural. "O Divine Love!" she exclaimed, "what is it You behold in this virgin which obliges You to esteem her so highly and to love her so much?" Our Lord replied: "*It is my goodness alone which obliges Me; since she contains and perfects in her soul those five virtues which please Me above all others and which I have placed therein by a singular liberality. She possesses purity, by a continual influence of My grace; she possesses humility, amidst the great diversity of gifts which I have bestowed on her—for the more I effect in her, the more she abases herself; she possesses a true benignity, which makes her desire the salvation of the whole world for My greater glory; she possesses a true fidelity, spreading abroad, without reserve, all her treasures for the same end. Finally, she possesses a consummate charity; for she loves Me with her whole heart, with her whole soul and with her whole strength; and for love of Me, she loves her neighbor as herself.*"

After Our Lord had spoken to this soul, He showed her a precious stone on His Heart, in the form of a triangle, made of trefoils, the beauty and brilliancy of which cannot be described, and He said to her:

"I always wear this jewel as a pledge of the affection which I have for My spouse. I have made it in this form, that all the celestial court may known by the brightness of the first leaf that there is no creature on earth so dear to Me as Gertrude, because there is no one at this present time among mankind who is united to Me so closely as she is, either by purity of intention or by uprightness of will. They will see by the second leaf that there is no soul still bound by the chains of flesh and blood whom I am so disposed to enrich by My graces and favors. And they will observe in the splendor of the third leaf that there is no one who refers to My glory alone the gifts received from Me with such sincerity and fidelity as Gertrude, who, far from wishing to claim the least thing for herself, desires most ardently that nothing shall be ever attributed to her." Our Lord concluded this revelation by saying to the holy person to whom He had thus condescended to speak of the perfections of our Saint:

"You cannot find Me in any place in which I delight more, or which is more suitable for Me, than in the Sacrament of the Altar, and after that, in the heart and soul of Gertrude, My beloved; for toward her all My affections, and the complacencies of My Divine love, turn in a singular manner."

On another occasion, a devout person who was praying for the Saint heard these words:

"She for whom thou prayest is My dove, who has no guile in her, for she rejects from her heart as gall all the guile and bitterness of sin. She is My chosen lily, which I love to bear in My hands, for it is My delight and My pleasure to repose in the purity and innocence of this chaste soul. She is My rose, whose odor is full of sweetness because of her patience in every adversity and the thanksgiving

which she continually offers Me, which ascend before Me as the sweetest perfumes. She is that spring flower which never fades, and which I take pleasure in contemplating because she keeps and maintains continually in her breast an ardent desire not only for all virtues, but for the utmost perfection of every virtue. She is as a sweet melody which ravishes the ears of the blessed; and this melody is composed of all the sufferings she endures with so much constancy."

…A sister who was touched by the devotion with which these words were uttered ['Thou shalt love the Lord thy God with thy whole heart, and with thy whole soul, and with thy whole strength" (Deut.6:5)]; prayed that He who so loved Gertrude and had taught her to love Him so much, would vouchsafe to impart to her the same blessed lesson. Our Lord replied:

"I have borne her in My arms from her infancy. I have preserved her in her baptismal purity and innocence, until she, by her own free choice and will, has given herself to Me entirely and forever; and as a recompense for the perfection of her desires, I, in return, have given Myself entirely to her. So pleasing is this soul to Me, that when I am offended by men, I often enter therein to repose, and I make her endure some pain of body or of mind, which I inflict on her for the sins of others; and as she accepts this suffering with the same thanksgiving, humility and patience as she receives all that comes from Me, and offers it to Me in union with My sufferings, she appeases My anger, and obliges My mercy to pardon, for her sake, an immense number of sinners."

On another occasion, Gertrude having humbly asked the prayers of a sister, the religious complied with her request and while praying for the Saint, heard these words:

"The faults which appear in Gertrude may rather be called steps in perfection, for it would be almost impossible that human weakness could be preserved from the blasts of vainglory, amidst the abundance of graces which I continually operate in her, if her virtues were not hidden from her eyes under the veils and shadows of apparent

defects. Thus, even as the earth produces a richer and more abundant harvest in proportion as the laborer has been careful in manuring it, so the gratitude of Gertrude bears Me richer fruit, the more I make her see her own weakness. It is for this reason that I permit different imperfections in her, for which she is in a state of continual humiliation, sending her a particular grace for each, with which she blots them all out from My sight; and the time will come when I change these defects into so many virtues, so that her soul will shine before Me as a most glorious sun."

Her deep study of Holy Scripture and of the Fathers now bore abundant fruit, and it was observed that she had a singular and Heaven-sent felicity in applying what she had read and treasured in her memory t the spiritual necessities of those with whom she conversed.

God and the salvation of souls—this was the one object of her life. From her humility, she had fully persuaded herself that the marvelous graces bestowed on her were given her merely for others. This holy delusion served two important ends—it saved her from every temptation to spiritual complacence, and it induced her to impart freely to others a knowledge of the revelations and other favors bestowed on her. She was simply, according to her own idea, a channel of divine grace to others; and believing this to be her end, she neither spared time nor labor for its accomplishment. Often her rest was shortened and her food forgotten when souls demanded time or anxious thought. "Not satisfied even with this, she often deprived herself of the sweetness of contemplation when it was necessary to succor the tempted, to console the afflicted, or, what she desired above all else, to enkindle and increase the fire of divine love in any soul. For as iron, when placed in the fire, becomes itself like fire, thus this virgin, burning with love, seemed to be all love, such zeal had she for the salvation of all."

Once after St. Gertrude had become Abbess of the convent, Our Lord appeared to her, bearing on His sacred shoulders a vast and magnificent building. "Behold," He said, "with what labor, care and vigilance I carry this beloved house, which is none other than that of Religion. It is everywhere threatened with ruin because there are so few persons who are willing to do or to suffer anything for its support and increase. You, therefore, should suffer with Me in bearing it; for all those who endeavor, by their words or actions, to extend religion, and who try to reestablish it in its first fervor and purity, are so many strong pillars which sustain this holy house and comfort Me by sharing with Me the weight of this burden.

Under her guidance, the fervent increased in fervor, and the saintly advanced rapidly in perfection. Many were favored with intimate and most blessed communications from Heaven; one at least, her sister in the flesh as well as in the spirit, obtained even on earth a recognition of her sanctity, and ranks amongst those who are invoked upon the Church's altars.

But the life of the young Abbess was not to be devoted exclusively to active service; and our Lord began now to teach her that exterior zeal should have its limits, however holy the end for which it labored; that contemplation was not only necessary for the individual soul, but also to promote the glory of God in others, since prayer alone may effect conversions and sanctifications, while active exertion, without its vivifying influence, is of little avail. A person to whom our Divine Lord had revealed His designs in regard to the Saint wrote thus to her:

"O blessed Spouse of Christ, enter into the joy of your Lord! His Divine Heart opens for you its fount of ineffable sweetness as a reward for the fidelity with which you have labored for His glory and for the defense of the truth. He desires now that you should rest in the shadow of His most peaceful consolations; for as a good tree planted by the riverside, takes root deeply and produces abundant fruit, so will you produce for your Beloved the fruit of your thoughts, words, and actions which are most pleasing to Him, by His grace operating within you. Do not fear that the heat of persecution will wither up your soul, for it is continually bedewed by the sacred waters of grace.

As you seek in all your actions the glory of God, and not your own, the fervor of your zeal increases a hundredfold the fruits which you offer to your dear Spouse, not only by the pious works which you actually accomplish, but even by those which you desire to do yourself or to see done by others, although it is not in your prayer to perform them. Jesus Christ Himself will supply before His Father your needs and your defects, and those of other for whom you are solicitous; therefore do not doubt that He will equally reward all you desire to do as if you had accomplished it, and know that the whole court of Heaven rejoices in your advancement, and return thanks and praise to God for love of you."

The Saint's confidence in God was indeed an eminent characteristic of her sanctity and one which obtained for her immense favors. How could the Heart of Jesus refuse anything to one who trusted Him so entirely? How pleasing this virtue was to her Spouse was revealed to one of her religious, who had long prayed in vain for a particular favor which she ardently desired. At last our Divine Lord vouchsafed to inform her of the reason for this delay, at which she had felt and expressed her profound amazement.

"I have delayed answering your prayers because you have not yet sufficient confidence in the effects which My mercy produces in you. Why do you not act like Gertrude, My chosen virgin, who is so firmly established on My Providence, that there is nothing which she does not hope for from the plenitude of My grace; therefore I will never refuse her anything, whatever she may ask of Me."

A holy man once earnestly prayed that he might know what virtue was most pleasing to Our Lord in His spouse. He was answered that it was "her generosity of heart." But as this surprised him not a little, he ventured to reply; "As for me, O Lord, I had imagined that what pleased You most in this soul was the perfect knowledge she had of herself, and the high degree of love to which, by Your grace, she has attained."

Our Lord replied:

"This generosity of heart is of such value and so great a good, that the height of perfection may be obtained through it. By means of it My elect is prepared at all times for receiving gifts of great value, which prevents her from attaching her heart to anything which could either impede Me or displease Me."

The happy manner in which she combined the duties of the active life with that unceasing union with her Beloved which so specially characterized her spiritual life was shown to St. Mechtilde in a vision. On one occasion, as she chanted, she beheld our Divine Lord seated on a high throne around which St. Gertrude walked without turning her eyes from her Master even for a moment. At the same time, she appeared to fulfill her exterior duties with the most perfect exactness. As her holy sister mused in amazement on the vision, she heard these words:

"This is an image of the life which My beloved Gertrude lives; thus does she ever walk in My presence, never relaxing in her ardent desire to know and to do what is most pleasing to My heart. As soon as she has ascertained it, she executes

it with care and fidelity, and then promptly passes to some other duty, seeking in her zeal always to find some new virtue to practice. Thus, her whole life is a continuous chain of praise, consecrated to My honor and glory."

"But Lord," replied St. Mechtilde, "if the life of St. Gertrude is so perfect, how is it that she cannot support the imperfections of others, and that they appear so great to her?"

Our Lord replied with admirable sweetness: *"It is because she cannot endure that her own heart should be sullied with the slightest stain, and therefore she cannot see without emotion the least defect in the heart of another."*

The sanctity of St. Mechtilde was well-known to the Saint, and she frequently asked her advice and prayers. Once, as Mechtilde fervently prayed for her, in compliance with her desire, she beheld our Divine Lord attired as a Bridegroom, and clothed in a robe of green lined with gold. His beauty surpassed that of millions of angels and He tenderly embraced with His right arm her for whom she prayed. It appeared to her that Gertrude also embraced her Lord, and that her heart was attached to the wound in the side of Jesus. As she sought in amazement to comprehend this extraordinary vision, she heard these words:

"Know that the green and gold of My vestments represent the operation of My Divinity, always new and always acting by the influence of My love. Yes...My operation is always new and always in action in the soul of Gertrude; and the union which you behold of her heart with My side shows that she is attached so inseparably to Me, that she is in a condition to receive every moment the infusions of My Divinity."

St. Mechtilde then asked if St. Gertrude, who was so dear to God, never committed any fault, and why she appeared so ready at any moment to change her occupation and to do, as if by chance, whatever came into her mind, her conscience appearing to be equally at rest whether she prayed, wrote, read, instructed, reproved, or consoled.

Our Savior replied:

"I have united My Heart so closely to her soul by the ties of My mercy that she has become one spirit with Me. It is on this account she obeys so promptly all the desires of My will, so that the harmony and understanding which exist between the different members of the body and the heart is not greater than that which exists between the soul of Gertrude and Mine; and as the moment a man has willed in his heart a movement of his hands, they accomplish his desire, because they are entirely subject to the will of the heart; and as one desires in his mind that his eyes should look on any object, and his eyes immediately open to obey him—so Gertrude is ever with Me, and at every moment is ready to obey the movements which I suggest."

St. Mechtilde once beheld the heart of the Saint forming, as it were, a firm and stable bridge, the sides of which appeared to her to be bordered, the one with the Divinity of Jesus Christ and the other with His holy Humanity, as with two walls. After beholding this, she heard these words:

"Those who come to Me by this bridge need have no apprehension of wandering or of falling; that is to say, all those who receive her counsels and execute them faithfully, shall never wander from the right path, which leads to the life of a blessed eternity."

When our Divine Lord revealed to the Saint that it was His Will she should commit her revelations to writing, her humility was exceedingly amazed. But her heavenly Spouse thus instructed and consoled her:

"For what purpose has it been committed to writing that I visited St. Catherine in her prison and encouraged her by these words: 'Be firm and immovable, My daughter, for I am with you'? What purpose does it serve that it should be known how I visited John, my favorite, and said to him, 'Come to Me, My beloved'? What purpose does it serve that these and many other things concerning them and others of My Saints are known, unless it be to enkindle the zeal of

those who read and hear them, and to manifest to all men the greatness of My love? In this manner, the desire of obtaining the same favors as those which they shall see you have obtained from Me will produce devotion in the hearts of those who, considering the effusion of My grace and the excess of My mercy, shall endeavor to change their present life for one more perfect."

On another occasion, as the Saint marveled why God urged her so strongly to make known her revelations, since He knew that the majority of mankind are so weak and unspiritual, that, far from finding in them any example for their edification, they would more probably find a subject of contempt, she heard the Lord saying to her:

"I have so planted My grace in you, that I expect it will bear Me immense fruit; therefore, it is My desire that all those who receive similar favors, and who despise them by their negligence, shall learn from you on what conditions I have given them these gifts, in order that My grace may be increased in them in proportion as their gratitude increases. But should there be any sufficiently malicious to defame the sanctity of these works, the penalty of their sin shall fall on themselves, and you will not be accountable for it. For the Prophet Ezechiel has said from Me: 'I will lay a stumbling block before him (Ez.3:20); that is to say, I dispose, permit, and even command many things for the salvation of My elect, although they are a subject of scandal to the reprobate."

A person to whom the Saint was entirely unknown, but who had been asked to pray for her, received the following communications from Our Lord:

"I delight so much in her that I have chosen her as My abode. Al that others see and love in her is My work, and whoever loves My work in her, loves Me; it is for this reason that those who are not capable of perceiving the interior gifts of her mind, admire her address, her eloquence, and all the

other exterior qualities with which I have endowed her. And I desire that they should know that I have withdrawn her from her parents and all her friends, that none may love her from ties of consanguinity, but that I Myself may be the only cause of the love and esteem which they have for her."

As the Saint was deprived for some time of the accustomed visits of her Spouse, she ventured to inquire why the favor was withheld, though she neither fell into discouragement nor depression in consequence.

Our Lord replied:

"When a person looks at anyone who is close to them, the too great proximity often prevents them from seeing distinctly; as, for example, when a friend meets his friend and embraces him, this close union deprives him of the pleasure of looking at him."

St. Gertrude understood by these words, that we often merit more when deprived of sensible grace, provided that we do not become less fervent in the practice of good works.

In the early years of the Saint's spiritual life, Our Lord often spoke to her in an audible voice, but later these communications assumed a different character. The Saint inquired the reason and received this reply:

"In former years I oftener instructed you by giving you various answers that you might know, and that you might make known, the designs of My will to others; but now I only make Myself known to you in spirit and I give you inspirations by lights which would be difficult to express in words. For I have chosen you for this purpose that I may use you as the repository of My treasures, wherein I may repose the riches of My grace, providing that everyone should find whatever he needs in you, as in the spouse who knows all the secrets of her Bridegroom, and on account of her Divine union with Him, acknowledges His wishes and His Will in all things."

And it was even so; for when the Saint prayed for anything, even if she received no reply from Our Lord as she had done formerly, she nevertheless felt equal consolation, and a certain assurance that her prayer was heard. Also, when anyone came to ask counsel or consolation of her, she at once felt her heart filled with the necessary light and inspired what to say, without a moment's reflection— and this was so much assurance and certainty, that she would have given her life for the truth of the inspiration.

As the religious, like a faithful and loving sister, offered the Host at the Elevation of her soul, with all the fidelity of the Heart of Jesus, she saw her elevated to a higher and yet more sublime degree of glory, where her garments shone marvelously and she was honored by blessed spirits. And this she beheld whenever she made this offering for her.

Then, as she inquired of our Divine Lord why the sister had appeared in great fear and alarm during her agony, she received this reply:

"It was for her good and an effect of My mercy. For during her sickness she desired very much to be assisted by your prayers, so that she might be admitted into Heaven immediately. I promised you this favor, which she believed she would obtain from Me. I was pleased with her confidence and determined to do her yet more good than I had before purposed. But as young persons seldom purify themselves from slight negligences; such as seeking too much amusement and taking pleasure in what is useless—and as it was necessary that she should be purified from these little stains by the inconveniences and pains of sickness, before I could bring her to Heaven, I could not bear that, after having endured all with so much resignation and patience she should still be unable to enjoy this blessedness. I therefore permitted her to be further tried by fear, caused by the sight of evil spirits; and thus she became perfectly purified and merited eternal glory."

'But where wert Thou, then, O Lord?' inquired the religious.

Our Lord replied:

I was hidden on her left side, and as soon as she was sufficiently purified. I showed Myself to her and took her with Me to eternal rest and glory.

BOOK III

(Excerpts from)   THE HERALD OF DIVINE LOVE

Prologue:

The grace of a great humility together with the power of the divine will were compelling her with a sort of urgency to make known to another person the confidences that follow. She thought she was herself so unworthy that her gratitude would not be a sufficient response to God's magnificent gifts. And so, when she had revealed them to another person, she rejoiced in God's praise, which, as it seemed to her, would then, like a precious stone, be lifted out of the dark mud and worthily set in gleaming gold. Finally, it was at the command of her superiors that this confidant wrote the following pages:

Chapter 2 – The Rings of the Spiritual Espousals

While she was offering to God in a short prayer all the pain she had to endure of body or soul, and all the joys, spiritual or physical, which were denied her, the Lord appeared. He was wearing this two-fold offering she had made him —namely, of joys and sufferings—in the form of two jeweled rings, one on each hand. When she had understood the meaning of this, she often repeated the samr prayer. After a little while, she was reciting it when she felt the Lord stroking her left eye with the wing on his left hand, which she understood to be a symbol of physical pain. And from that time, that same eye which she had seen the Lord touching spiritually, suffered so much physically that it never regained its former health. From this she understood that just as the ting is the symbol of espousals, so any trial, whether of body or soul, is the truest sign of divine election and is like the espousals of the soul with God; so that those who suffer can say truly, and even with confidence: "My Lord Jesus Christ has espoused me with a ring." And so in all her adversities she never lacked this gift of grace, and she could truly raise her mind in grateful praise and thanksgiving to God and in consequence could joyfully add these words: "And like a being adorned me with a crown." Gratitude in adversity is like being adorned with the most beautiful crown of glory, more precious far than gold and topaz (Ps. 118:127).

Chapter 4 – Contempt for Temporal Comforts

Around the feast of St. Bartholomew she was overwhelmed by inordinate sadness and impatience; her soul was invaded by such darkness that it seemed to her that he had almost entirely lost the joy of the divine presence. This lasted until the following Saturday when she had the happiness of seeing the darkness disperse through the intervention of the Virgin Mother of God during the singing of the antiphon "Stella Maris Maria" in her honor.

Next day, in her joy at being so caressed and cherished through the goodness of God, she remembered her previous impatience and all her of her defects. She began to be very dissatisfied with herself and, in a spirit of dejection—indeed, almost despair, so many and so great were the defects which she discovered within herself—she besought the Lord to help her to improve, in these words: "Alas, most merciful Lord, make an end to my wickedness, for I know not how to correct it or to put an end to it. Deliver me, O Lord, and set me beside thee, and let any man's hand fight against me" (Job 17:3).

Taking pity on her desolation, the merciful Lord showed her a very small and extremely narrow garden, where flowers of various kinds were growing in profusion. It was surrounded by a hedge of thorns and a feeble trickle of honey was flowing through it. And he said to her: "Would you prefer the pleasure you take in these pretty flowers to me?" "Never, Lord God!" she answered. Then he showed her a little garden with muddy soil, covered with unattractive greenery interspersed with a few worthless but fairly colorful little flowers. He questioned her about this as well, saying: "Now, would you prefer this one to me?" She turned away from it indignantly and answered: "Far be it from me to prefer what is false and worthless (I do not call it good but positively bad) to you, the only true, the supreme, solid, lasting and eternal good!" He said: "Why then, this lack of confidence, as though you were not in charity, although anyone who has received such an abundance of gifts must surely be convinced of it? Does not Scripture bear witness that charity covers a multitude of sins (1 Pet 4:8)? That is why you do not prefer you own will to mine, when you could live without any adversity, comfort-ably and honorably, finding favor with men and with a reputation for great holiness. Now I showed you this in the similitude of the flower garden, and I set before you the pleasures of the life of the flesh in the verdure of this muddy place." To which she rejoined: "Oh, I wish a thousand times I wish, that I had entirely renounced my will in despising the flower garden which you showed me; but I am afraid that the narrowness of the garden led me too easily to reject it." And the Lord said: "But it is my overflowing love for my chosen ones that makes me usually restrict their temporal satisfactions and comforts through the pricklings of conscience, so that they may the more easily despise them."

Then she proceeded with constancy to renounce all pleasure, both heavenly and earthly. Reposing on the breast of her Beloved, cleaving firmly to him, it seemed to her that no creature would be powerful enough to remove her, ever so little, from this refuge where she was always ready to draw with joy (Is 12:3) from the Lord's side and taste of the flood of life-giving sweetness, far surpassing the sweetness of balm.

Chapter 6 – The Soul's Cooperation with God

On the feast of St. Maurice while Mass was being celebrated and the priest was proceeding to the silent words of the consecration of the host, she said to the Lord: "This act, Lord, that you are about to perform deserves a perfect and infinite respect; and that is why, I, who am so insignificant, dare not even raise my eyes to it. Rather, I shall plunge myself down and lie in the deepest valley of humility I can find, there to await my portion of it; for from it comes the salvation of all the elect."

To which the Lord answered: "When a mother wants to do some embroidery with silk or pearls, sometimes she puts her little one in a higher place to hold the thread of pearls or help her in some other way. And so I have put you in a higher place with the intention of making you participate in this Mass. Because, if you will raise yourself up to help me of your own free will in this work, even if it is hard; if you want to be of service so that this oblation may have its full effect on all Christians, whether living or dead, in accordance with its dignity and excellence; then you will have given me the best possible help in my work, according to your possibilities."

…She said, "All the same Lord, are you not going to hear me when I pray for any of my friends" To which the Lord replied, as though confirming it with an oath: "By my divine power, I shall certainly do so!" And she replied: "Then I shall pray now for that person who has been so often recommended to me." At once she saw a little river, pure as crystal, issuing from the Lord's breast and flowing into the heart of the person for whom she was praying. Then she questioned the Lord, saying: "Lord, as this person does not feel the influx of grace, what good can it do her?" To which the Lord answered: "When a doctor makes a sick person drink a cup of medicine, it is not when the person swallows the draught that those who are looking after him can see that he is restored to health; neither does the sick person feel at once that he is cured, and yet the doctor, who knows the healing power of draught of medicine, knows very well in what way it will be beneficial to the sick person." And she said: "Why, Lord, do you not take away her unreasonable ways and other defects about which I have so often prayed to you?" To which the Lord said: "It was said of me, the child Jesus: 'And Jesus advanced in age and wisdom before God and man (lk 2:52). This person grows gradually and improves from hour to hour; she will turn her vices into virtues. I will forgive her all her human failings so that she may see after this life all that I have prepared for man in decreeing to exalt him above the angels."

Now the time was approaching when she was to go to communion. She asked of the Lord that, in addition to the number of souls which he was that day to release from their pains to join the heavenly choirs through the prayers of the person who has been several times mentioned, he would also anticipate the hour of his grace for the same number of sinners who were destined to be saved. She did not presume to pray for those who were destined to be damned, but the Lord chided her for her timidity, and said: "Surely the dignity of the presence of my immaculate body and of my precious blood is such that even those who are in a state of mortal sin might through its merits be recalled to a better way of life?" Pondering on the extent of the generosity in these words, she said: "Since your inestimable love condescends to hear my unworthy words," she said, "I implore your Majesty, in union with the love and desire of all your creatures, that, whatever the number of souls may be which you will now release from purgatory, you may grant me that the same number of sinners still living in this world in a state of mortal sin may attain to your grace—those for whom you particularly desire prayers to be offered. Let it be granted to whomever you desire, at any time and in any place. I do not choose to pray specially for my friends or relatives or those near me." This the kind Lord graciously accepted and gave her his assurance about it."

Then she said: "I would like to know, Lord, what it would please you that I should add to these prayers." Receiving no reply to this, she said: "I know Lord, that in my unfaithfulness I do not deserve to receive a reply to this question, because you, to whom all hearts are known, know me to be so negligent that perhaps I would not do as you tell me." The Lord with a serene countenance tenderly replied: "Confidence alone is sufficient to obtain everything easily; but if in your devotion you really desire to add something over and above, then recite the psalm 'O praise the Lord all ye nations' (Ps. 116) three hundred-sixty-five times to make up for any negligences of theirs in my divine praise.

There is no doubt that she was one of his elect, one of those blessed ones of whom St. Bernard has written in his sermons on the Song, saying: "I think that a soul in a state of grace is not only heavenly on account of its origin, it is even not unworthy itself to be called heaven on account of its imitation of heaven; it is heaven in its manner of life." It is of souls like these that it is written in the Book of Wisdom: "The soul of the just is the throne of wisdom (Prov 12:23). And again: "Heaven is my throne" (Is 66:1). As he knows that God is a spirit, therefore he has no hesitation in ascribing to him a spiritual throne. I am confirmed in this belief by the true promise: "To him (that is, the holy man), we shall come and shall make our dwelling with him" (Jn 14:23). The prophet was making the same point when he said: "But thou dwellest in a holy place, the praise of Israel" (Ps 21:4)....

Oh, how great is the breadth of that soul and how glorious are the merits of her who was within her the power of the divinity, and who is found worthy of receiving him and able to contain him, in whom there is room enough for the fulfillment of the work of his Majesty. She grew into the holy temple of the Lord; she grew, I say, in the measure of charity, which is the dimension of the soul. Therefore, in the heaven of this holy soul she has her intellect as a sun, faith as a moon, and virtues as stars. Certainly the sun of this soul is the sun of justice or the fervor of burning charity, and the moon is continence. Nor is it surprising that the Lord Jesus willingly dwells in this heaven. This soul was not like others; he did not merely speak so as to create it, but he fought to win it, and he laid down his life t redeem it. After his labors, as he saw his desire fulfilled, he said: "This is my rest for ever and ever; here will I dwell, for I have chosen it" (Ps 131:14).

And now, to show to the best of my feeble ability that she is of the number of thoe blessed ones of whom St. Bernard says that God has chosen them for his dwelling in preference to the physical heavens for his glory. I shall relate what a spiritual friendship of many years has enabled me to know. St. Bernard says frequently that the spiritual heaven, that is, the holy soul which is become a worthy dwelling for the Lord, should be adorned not by the sun, the moon, and the stars, but by the beauty of the virtues. Now I shall show briefly and as best I can what those virtues are which shone in her with special brilliance, that there may be no doubt that the Lord of might and power had his dwelling within her, because of the beauty which radiated from her, shone around, and so wonderfully adorned even her outward appearance.

Chapter 7 – Her Zeal for the Salvation of Souls

Her words and deeds provide the clearest evidence of her great zeal for souls and her love of religion. When she saw some defect in the soul of another, she longed for the person to correct it; if she did not see any improvement, she was inconsolate until she was able to bring this about, at least in some measure, by her prayers to God, her exhortations, or the help of another person. If, as is but human, someone, bt way of consolation, happened to say that she should not trouble about a person who would not correct himself, because he would atone for it by paying the due penalty, she felt as much pain as though a sword had pierced her heart and said she would rather choose death than have consolation in the face of a person's fault when he would feel the force of it only after his death and would have to pay the penalty of eternal damnation.

When she found in Holy Scripture certain passages which she thought woud be of use, if they seemed to her to be too difficult for persons of lesser intelligence, she would translate them into simpler language so that they might be of greater profit to their readers. She passed her life from morning to night with the sacred texts, either abridging long passages or explaining difficult ones, to the glory

of God which she so much desired and for the salvation of others. The beauty of this work is well described by Bede: "What occupation more sublime or more pleasing to God could there be than to take one's daily study to convert others to the grace of their Creator and to add to the total number of faithful souls ever increasing the joys of heaven?" And by Bernard: "The characteristic of true and chaste contemplation is that the soul, aflame with divine fire, conceives such a vehement desire to attract other souls to God to love him equally, that it gladly leaves the leisure of contemplation with an ardor that is all the greater for being able to take into consideration the fruits of its labors. And if, being able to take into consideration the fruits of its labors." And if, according to Gregory, there is no sacrifice which gives so much praise to God as zeal for the salvation of souls, it is not surprising that the Lord Jesus should have deigned to lay himself voluntarily upon his living altar, whence the pleasing odor of such a precious offering mounts ceaselessly toward him.

Once the Lord Jesus, fairest of all the children of men, appeared to her. He was standing and bearing on his princely shoulders the weight of a house of very great size which seemed about to fall in ruins. The Lord aid to her: "See the effort I am making to support this house of my holy religion, which I love so much. All over the world this house is threatened with ruin because so very few people are to be found willing to work faithfully or to suffer in its defense and for its expansion. Look at me, then, beloved and have compassion on my weariness….All those who promote religion by word or deed are like columns supporting my burden and they help me to bear it in proportion to their powers." Profoundly moved by these words, she was filled with compassion for God, her beloved Lord, and she resolved to work still harder for the advancement of religion. In observing the Rule, she even went beyond her strength in order to give a good example.

Chapter 13 – Some Miracles

In the month of March, the cold was so intense that the lives of humans as well as of animals were threatened. She heard the people say that this year would be no harvest, because according to the phases of the moon the cold weather was going to last a long time. One day at Mass when she was going to communion she was devoutly praying to the Lord for this intention and for many other graces as well. When she had finished her prayer, she received this reply from the Lord: "Be certain that all the intentions for which you have prayed will be granted." To which she responded: "Lord, if I am certain of being heard, and if it is therefore right to thank you, show me a proof by mitigating the rigor of the cold weather." That said, she thought no more about it, but when Mass was over and she was coming out of Choir, she found the path quite flooded by the melting of the frozen ice and snow. Those who saw this change, contrary to the laws of nature were astonished. As they did not know that God's chosen one had obtained the thaw by her prayers, they repeated, that alas, it would not last, as it was contrary to the ordinary course of nature. However, the thaw was followed by fine spring weather which continued for the whole season.

Another time, in the harvest season, it was raining continuously and everyone was praying for fear of losing the harvest. She, joining with the others, offered such efficacious and insistent prayers to placate the Lord that she obtained from him a formal promise, that for her sake, he would moderate the intemperate weather. This took place the same day. Although the sky had been covered with clouds, the sun came out and the splendor of its rays shone over the whole earth.

However, that evening, the community had gone out to do some work in the courtyard. The sun was still shining splendidly, but rain clouds were to be seen gathering in the sky. I heard her say to the Lord, with a deep and heartfelt sigh: "O Lord, God of the universe, I do not want to compel you to obey my unworthy will, but rather, if it is for my sake that, in your infinite goodness, you are keeping back the rain, and if it is contrary to what would be in accordance with your strict justice, I ask you to release it instantly, that your adorable will may be done." Wonderful to relate, as soon as she had finished speaking, the weather broke and there was a violent thunderstorm with heavy raindrops. Stupefied, she said to the Lord, "O most merciful God, if it pleases your goodness, keep back the rain until we have finished this work which we are doing in obedience to our instructions." At this petition the kind Lord held back the thunderstorm until the community had finished the work they had been told to do. As soon as it was finished and while they were still outside, rain began to fall and there was a violent storm with flashes of lightning and peals of thunder, so that those who still remained in the courtyard were completely frenched.

Yet another time she was praying to the Lord about the winds which were drying up everything and she received this response: "Sometimes I need a reason for hearing the prayers of my chosen ones, but between you and me no reason is necessary; through my grace, your will is united with mine and you cannot will anything except as I will. I shall tell you, then, that I want this bad weather in order that some rebellious people may be forced to pray to me, at least for this intention. And so, I shall not grant your prayer, but instead I shall give you some spiritual gift in exchange." Hearing this, she gladly agreed, and thenceforth she always rejoiced on such occasions if her prayers could be heard in no other way than that which was pleasing to God. St. Gregory says that the proof of sanctity is not in performing miracles, but in loving others as oneself, and of this we have already spoken at sufficient length.

Chapter 14 – Special Privileges Granted Her by God

I must add here some other characteristic anecdotes of the same kind. I had as much trouble unearthing them as if they had been buried beneath a great stone. I have included also some eyewitness accounts which I have from people of the greatest reliability.

Several people came to consult her in their doubts and difficulties, especially to ask her whether, for one reason or another, they should abstain from going to Holy Communion. After having given some wise counsel to each, she exhorted them to go to the Lord's sacrament, trusting in God's mercy and grace, and sometimes she almost compelled them. Once, however, as usually happens sooner or later to every sincere soul, she began to fear that her advice was more presumptuous than was right. She turned to God, trusting in his customary mercy and love, and disclosed her fears. This was the consoling response: "Be not afraid, but be consoled, take comfort, and be secure, because I am the Lord God your Lover who made you for myself out of pure love and chose you as a dwelling-place wherein to find my pleasure. Without doubt, I give a rue answer to those who ask of me through you, humbly and devoutly. You may take this as a certain promise: I shall never permit anyone whom I consider unworthy to partake of the life-giving sacrament of my body and blood to question you about it. If, therefore, I send some weary and afflicted soul to you to be comforted, say to whomever it may be to come with confidence to receive me. Because of the love and the grace I give you, I shall not exclude them from my fatherly care, but I shall extend to them my most affectionate embrace and I shall not deny them my sweet kiss of peace."

Afterward, when she was praying for someone, she was afraid this person hoped to obtain through her intercession more than she could have obtained for herself. The Lord very kindly replied: "Whatever people aspire to obtain through your intervention, they will certainly receive. Moreover, I shall most certainly give them everything which you have promised in my name; even if they are prevented by human frailty from feeling the effects of it, I shall work in their soul to bring about the perfection you had promised them."

After some weeks had passed, remembering these words of the Lord and unable to forget their own unworthiness, she asked the Lord how he could perform such wonders by means of a creature so base. The Lord replied: "Does not the whole church possess what I promised only to Peter, when I said: 'And whatsoever thou shalt bind upon earth, it shall be bound also in heaven?' (Matt 16:19). The church believes that this same power still resides in all her ministers. Why do you not believe that, prompted by love, I can and will perform whatever I have personally promised to do?" He touched her tongue, saying: "Behold, I have given my words in thy mouth (Jer 1:9). And in truth I confirm all the words which, inspired by my Spirit, you shall speak for me. And whatsoever you promise on earth, relying on my goodness, I shall ratify in heaven." To this she objected: "Lord, I should be unhappy if someone suffered damnation because the Spirit obliged me to tell him that his sin could not go unpunished, or something of the kind." The Lord replied: "If you say such a thing for justice's sake or through zeal for souls, I shall surround that person with my merciful love and induce him to feel compunction, so that he will not merit my vengeance." Then she asked the Lord: "Lord, if you really speak with my mouth, as you have just told me in your loving kindness that you do, how is it that sometimes the words which I speak with so much desire for your glory and for the salvation of souls have so little effect?" To which the Lord answered: "Do not be surprised that your words are at times spoken in vain, since I myself during my earthly life often preached with all the fervor of my divine Spirit and yet with certain people, my words had no effect. Everything comes to pass in time by my divine ordinance."

Another day she was praying for some people who had been recommended to her and she received this answer from the Lord: "In former times, anyone who could touch the corner of the altar could rejoice in having found sanctuary (3 Kings 1:31;2:28), since in my gracious condescension I have deigned to choose you for a dwelling, anyone who commits himself with confidence to your prayers will be saved by my grace."

For this we have the testimony of Dame M., the chantress of sweet memory, When she was praying one day for the soul of whom we write, she was shown to her in her heart in the likeness of a very solid bridge, supported on one side by the humanity of Jesus Christ and on the other by his divinity, as though by a wall. She heard the Lord say: "None of those who try to come to me by this bridge can fall or go astray." That is to say, none of those who hear her words and obey her injunctions will ever be lost.

Chapter 15 – How the Lord Compelled Her to Publish These Favors

After this the Lord gave her to understand that it was his will that the story of these graces should be put down in writing for others to read. She asked herself wonderingly what good there could be in this: for in her heart she had firmly decided that she would never permit any of it to be known during her lifetime, and it seemed to her that if it were published after her death it would only cause trouble by disturbing the minds of the faithful, who would realize that they could now derive no profit from it. The Lord answered her thoughts thus: "And what good do you think it does to read that when I was visiting blessed Catherine in prison I say to her: "Be of good cheer, daughter, for I am with you! Or when I called my special apostle John and said: 'Come to me, my beloved!' Or the many other things which one reads of thee and of others? Is it not that devotion is increased in this way, serving as a reminder of my love for human beings?" And the Lord added: "When they hear about these graces that you have received, others may be brought to desire for them for themselves, and by thinking about them, they may try somewhat to amend their lives.

On another occasion she was wondering why the Lord had been insisting for so long within her spirit that she should publish what is written in this book, for she was not unaware of the fact that some people have such small hearts that gifts such as hers would often be despised and could become a pretext for calumny rather then for edification. The Lord instructed her in this way: "I have poured out my grace in your heart because I require great profit from it. That is why I want those who have received gifts similar to yours and who are careless enough to underestimate their value and make light of them to read about you; then they can recognize their own gifts and grow in gratitude and so increase in grace themselves. As for those with hearts so evil that they should want to calumniate my gifts, may their sins be on their own heads, while you remain blameless as the Prophet said by my inspiration: 'I will lay a stumbling block before them'' (Ez 3:20). These words made her understand that sometimes God makes his saints do things which are a source of scandal to others. The elect should not fail to do these things in the hope of making peace with perverse people, because true peace consists in overcoming evil with good (Rom 12:21). That is, while we should not omit anything that may give glory to God, we should placate perverse people with kindness, for in this way do we gain our neighbor (Matt 18:15). If this does not succeed, we will not lose our reward. Hugh says: "As the faithful can always find a reason for doubting, if they wish, so unbelievers can find a reason for believing;

it is with justice that the faithful are rewarded for their faith, and unbelievers punished for their incredulity."

Chapter 16 – In Revelations to Others, the Lord Gives Clear Proof of the Truth of Hers

When she reflected on her wretched and worthless state, she thought she was quite unworthy of such great gifts as those with which she knew God was constantly enriching her. She went to Dame Mechthild of happy memory, who was held in great esteem and honor for her grace of revelations. She humbly begged her to ask the Lord about the gifts mentioned above, not because she wanted to arouse in herself a greater sense of gratitude and to be confirmed in faith, lest afterward she should be led to doubt by her sense of her extreme unworthiness. Dame Mechthild, as she had been asked, took counsel with the Lord in prayer.

She saw the Lord Jesus as a Spouse, full of grace and vigor, fairer than a thousand angels. He was clad in green garments that seemed to be lined with gold. And she for whom she had prayed was being tenderly enfolded by his right arm, so that her left side, where the heart is, was held close to the opening of the wound of love; she for her part was seen to be enfolding him in the embrace of her left arm. Full of wonderment, blessed Mechthild desired to know what the meaning of this vision might be.

The Lord said to her: "Know that the green color of my garments lined with gold signifies that my divine works are ever green and flourishing. And this close proximity of her heart to mine that she is able to receive, directly and at all times, the flow of my divinity."

Again, she asked: "My Lord, is it true that you have given your chosen one such gifts that she can with certainty solve, according to the truth of your judgment, the problems of those who desire her help for any reason, and that those who seek the way of salvation through her will find it She has disclosed to me the words in which you deigned to make this promise to her, humbly coming to me for instruction." To which the Lord replied with great kindness: "Certainly I have given her these special privileges so that everyone can hope to obtain without any doubt all that he desires through her intervention. I shall never reckon as unworthy those whom she judges to be worthy of communion. I shall, indeed regard with particular affection those whom she urges to go to communion; also, she will judge the faults of those who come to consult her as grave or slight according to my divine discernment. And as there are three who bear witness in heaven, the Father, the Word, and the Holy Spirit (1 Jn 5:6), she should always base her decisions on a threefold assurance:

First, when she has to speak to other people, she should be aware of the interior inspirations of the Spirit. Second, she should consider whether the persons to whom she speaks are sorry for their fault, or want to be sorry for it. Third, she should consider whether they show good will. If these three signs are present, she should reply without hesitation in the way she thinks best and I will ratify whatever she promises in the name of my merciful love." And the Lord added: "Each time she wants to speak with others, she should draw into her soul a deep breath of inspiration from my divine heart. Whatever she says will then be spoken with certainty; neither she nor those who hear her can be deceived, because the secret intentions of my divine heart will be revealed in her words. May she keep faithful testimony of your words, and if, with the passage of time and among many different occupations she should think she feels my grace growing cold in her soul, as sometimes happens, she must not lose her trust, because I shall undoubtedly preserve the gift of these privileges in her as long as she lives."

Dame Mechthild asked the Lord whether her conduct were not perhaps rather reprehensible because she always hastened to do whatever came into her head; and how it was that it was all the same to her and no trouble to her conscience whether she prayed, read, wrote, gave instruction, corrected, or consoled others (Rom 14:8).

The Lord replied: "I have deigned to join my heart so courteously and so inseparably with her soul that she is become one spirit with me (1Cor 6:17) and her will is always in perfect harmony with my own in all things and above all things, just as the members of the body are in harmony among themselves and with the will. When a man thinks in his mind and says to his hand: Do this, at once the hand moves to perform the action. Again he says: Look at that, and at once the eyes open without delay. Thus, through my grace, she is always intent on asking me what I want her to do. For I have chosen to dwell in her in such a way that her will and the works which stem from this good will, are so firmly fixed in my heart that she is, as it were, the right hand with which I work. Her understanding is ike my own eye with which she perceives what pleases me; the movement of her spirit is like my own tongue, sinc, inspired by the Spirit, she says what I intend to be said. And her discretion is ike my nostrils, for I incline the ears of my mercy toward those for whom she is moved to compassion. And her attention is like feet for me, because she is always bent on going where it is fitting for me to follow. Therefore, it is necessary for her to be always hurrying, according to te promptings of my Spirit, so that as soon as she has finished one thing, she may be ready to begin another at my bidding. And if in doing this she has to neglect something, her conscience is never troubled, because by doing my will she makes up for it in some other way."

Another time, Gertrude besought Dame Mechthild to petition the Lord for her, especially for the virtues of gentleness and patience, of which she thought she had much need. Praying as she had been asked, Mechthild received this answer from the Lord: "The gentleness which pleases me in her takes its name from 'dwelling with' or 'indwelling.' And because I swell in her soul, she should be like a young bride who enjoys the presence of her spouse all the time, and if she must go out, she takes him by the hand and makes him follow her. And so each time that she finds it necessary to leave the repose of interior enjoyment to gain profit by instructing others, she must first make the sign of the cross of salvation on her breast and call upon my name, just that one word, and the, in my grace, she can confidently say whatever occurs to her. The patience which pleases me in her takes its name from "peace" and "science" or "knowledge; and such is her diligence in acquiring the virtue of patience that even in adversity she does not lose the peace of her heart, but always patiently strives to remember why it is that she suffers. Of course it is out of love that she does it as a sign of true fidelity."

Another person, a man to whom she was entirely unknown except that she had recommended herself to his prayers was praying for her and received this answer: "I have chosen to dwel in her because it delights me to see that everything that people love in her is my own work. Those who know nothing of interior that is, spiritual things, love in her at least my exterior gifts, such as intelligence, eloquence and so on. Therefore, I have exiled her from all her relatives, so that there should be no one who would love her for the sake of the ties of blood, and that I may be the only reason why all her friends love her."

"The sixth of your generous gifts, kindest Lord, is one more necessary to me than ay other. You gave me the assurance that anyone who would have the charity to pray faithfully for me, the most worthless of God's creatures, for the amendment of the sins and ignorance of my youth (Ps 24:7)—indeed, my malice and wickedness—whether by reciting prayers or by doing good works, would receive as a reward of your generous love the assurance that he would not leave this world without being given such grace that his conduct would be so pleasing to you that you would have the joy of a specially close friendship with his soul. In this you show your fatherly love and my dire necessity. You know how much and in how many ways, I need to amend my innumerable faults and negligences. In your merciful love, you do not want me to perish. On the other hand, in your admirable justice, you could not allow me to be saved with so many perfections. At least you have provided for me that, by my sharing in the gain of many, the share of each might increase.

In your extravagant generosity, kindest Lord, you added that if anyone knowing of the familiar companionship with which you have treated me, in my nothingness, during my lifetime, should humbly commend himself to my unworthy intercession after my death, you would without doubt deign to hear him as readily as you would ever grant the desire of anyone through the intercession of any other person; if, in reparation for his past negligence, he offer you thanks with humble devotion, especially for five graces.

The first is the love with which, in your merciful kindness, you chose me from all eternity. I can truthfully say that this is of all graces the most freely given. For you could not have been ignorant of how perverse my conduct would be, nor all of the details of my malice and wickedness and the baseness of my ingratitude. You might justly have denied me the honor due to human reason, even among pagans, but in your love which so greatly exceeds our misery you have chosen to confer on me, of all Christians, the dignity of being consecrated a religious.

The second is that you have drawn me to yourself for my salvation. And I am bound to confess that I owe this to the gentleness and goodness of your nature. You have won this rebellious heart of mine (which in all justice deserves to be bound in iron chains), drawing it to yourself by your sweet caresses as though you found me a fit consort for your gentleness and were quite delighted by your union with me.

The third is that you have so intimately united yourself with me. And this I ca but attribute to your overflowing, immense and boundless generosity. As though the number of the just were not sufficiently great to occupy your great love, you have called me, the least deserving of all, not in order to justify more easily the most suitable, but so that the miracle of your condescension might be reflected with greater brilliance in the least suitable.

Fourth, that you should take pleasure in this union. This I cam only ascribe to the folly of your love, if I may dare to speak in this way. As you have yourself asserted, you find your happiness in some incredible way in uniting your infinite wisdom with a being so unlike you and so unfitted for such a union.

Fifth, you are leading me graciously toward a blessed end. I humbly and firmly believe that I shall receive this gift from you, in the sweet kindness of your beneficient love, according to your faithful promise and despite my great unworthiness; and I embrace it with unshakable love and gratitude. It is not through any merit of mine, but solely through the free gift of your mercy, O my all, my supreme, my only true, eternal Good!

"Now the time was approaching when she was to go to communion. She asked of the Lord, that in addition to the number of souls which he was that day to release from their pains to join the heavenly choirs through the prayers of the person who has been several times mentioned, he would also anticipate the hour of his grace for the same number of sinners who were destined to be saved. She did not presume to pray for those who were destined to be damned, but the Lord chided her for her timidity, and said: "Surely the dignity of the presence of my immaculate body and of my precious blood is such that even those who are in a state of mortal sin might through its merits be called to a better way of life?" Pondering on the extent of the generosity in these words, she said: "Since your inestimable love condescends to hear my unworthy prayers. I implore your Majesty, in union with the love and desire of all your creatures, that, whatever the number of souls may be which you will now release from purgatory, you may grant me that the same number of sinners still living in this world in a state of mortal sin may attain to your grace—those for whom you particularly desire prayers to be offered. Let it be granted to whomever you desire, at any time, and in any place. I do not choose to pray specially for my friends or relatives or those near me." This the kind Lord graciously accepted and gave her his assurance about it.

Then she said: "I would like to know, Lord, what it would please you that I should add to these prayers." Receiving no reply to this, she said: "I know, Lord, in my unfaithfulness I do not deserve to receive a reply to this question, because you, to whom all hearts are known, know me to be so negligent that perhaps I would not do as you tell me." The Lord with a serene countenance tenderly replied: "Confidence alone is sufficient to obtain everything easily; but if in your devotion you really desire to add something over and above, then recite the psalm, 'O praise the Lord all ye nations' (Ps 116) three hundred sixty-five times to make up for any negligence of theirs in my divine praise."

On another occasion, at a similar hour and in the ame manner, the divine Love invited her to taste of his gentle sweetness with these words: "Observe the smallness of the material form in which I show you the whole of my divinity and my humanity, and compare this size with the size of the human body; judge, then, to what extent I stoop in my benevolence; for just as the size of the human body exceeds the size of my body—that is, my body under the species of bread—it is my mercy and my charity which induce me in this sacrament to permit the loving soul in some sort to prevail over me."

On another day, when the saving host was being distributed in communion, the Lord explained to her once again his exceedingly great condescension in these words: "Don't you see how the priest who is distributing the hosts has taken care to turn back the sleeves of the vestment he is wearing out of reverence for the sacrament while he celebrates and handles my body with his bare hands? I want you to understand that although, as is but right, I look with affection on the works done for my sake, such as prayers, fasts, vigils, and the like—however—though it does not seem so to the less spiritually minded—I am drawn toward my Elect with greater compassion when they are forced by their human weakness to have recourse to my mercy, just as you see that the bare flesh of the priest's hand touches me more closely than do his vestments."

When, on another day, the bell was sounding for communion and the chant was being intoned, she, feeling herself insufficiently prepared, said to the Lord: ""O my Lord, you are coming to me! Why did you not send me, as you easily could, some ornament of devotion with which I might come to you becomingly prepared?" To which the Lord replied: "Sometimes the Spouse is better pleased at seeing the fair neck of his bride unadorned than when it is covered by a necklace; and he is more pleased also to take her delicate and lovely hands (Song 5:14) in his own than to see them overed by long gloves. So I sometimes take more pleasure in an act of humility than in the grace of devotion."

When on another occasion she saw a different person very timid and fearful for the same reason, she began to pray for her. The Lord said: "I wish my chosen ones did not think me so cruel, but would believe that I accept as good, or even perfect, every act which costs them something. For example, it involves a personal sacrifice to carry out the worship due to God if one feels no sweetness of devotion, and yet serves him nonetheless by the recitation of prayers, by genuflections, and the like, and above all, trusts in his loving mercy. This homage God will be pleased to accept."

Again, praying for someone who was complaining that she received the grace of devotion much less frequently on the days when she went to communion than on certain other days, even ferial days, the Lord gave her this answer: "That is no accident, but comes about by my providence: because when on ferial days and also at unexpected moments it happens that I favor the soul with the grace of devotion. I intend thus to raise her up to me, when perhaps she would otherwise have remained in a state of tepidity. But when, on the other hand, on feast days or at the moment of communion, I withdraw this grace, the hearts of my chosen ones are more stimulated by voluntary desires or by humility, and this effort of attention or this contrition is often of more advantage to their salvation than os the grace of devotion.

The following day, as she was praying in this way, the Virgin Mother appeared to her in the presence of her ever adorable Trinity which appeared in the form of a fleur-e-lys, as it is usually shown, with three petals, one erect and two turning downward. Thus she was given to understand that the blessed Mother of God is justly called the White Lily of the Trinity, because she has received into herself, more fully and perfectly than any other creature, the virtues of the adorable Trinity; virtues which she never staned with even the least speck of venial sin. The erect petal denotes omnipotence of God the Father; the two turning downward, the Wisdom and Love of the Son and the Holy Spirit, whom she most resembles. Wherefore she understood from the blessed Virgin that if one were to salute her devoutly with the words: "White Lily of the Trinity and fairest Rose of heavenly bliss," she would show how great is her power through the omnipotence of the Father; and with what ingenuity she knows how to work for the salvation of the human race, through the wisdom of the Son; and how immeasurably her heart abounds in tenderness, through the love of the Holy Spirit.

The Blessed Virgin added: "Besides this, at the hour of death, I shall appear to the soul who salutes me in this way in a blossoming of such beauty that she will be wondrously consoled as I reveal to her the bliss of heaven. From that time Gertrude resolved to salute the blessed Virgin or her images with these words: "Hail, white Lily of the resplendent and ever tranquil Trinity! Fairest Rose of heaven's bliss! The King of Heaven chose to be born of you, to be fed with your milk! Oh, feed our souls on the outpourings of divine grace!"

Once when she was reflecting on the adversities of her past life, she asked the Lord why he had allowed her to be troubled by certain persons. To that she received the following reply: "When a fatherly hand is raised to chastise the child, the rod cannot resist. And o I could wish that my chosen ones would never blame the persons by whom they are tried, but should always consider that, in my fatherly affection, I would never let the faintest breath of wind blow against them if I were not looking to the eternal salvation they will receive as their reward; rather let them have compassion on those who stain their own souls for their purification."

One day she was having difficulty with a certain task and she said to God the Father: "Lord, I offer you this work through your only Son, in the power of the Holy Spirit to your eternal praise." She knew the power of these words to be such that in a marvelous way they elevate any work done with that intention far beyond human estimation, so that whatever is offered is made pleasing to God the Father. Just as that which is seen through a red glass and so on, whatever is offered to God the Father through His only-begotten Son becomes most pleasing and acceptable to Him.

Once as she was praying she asked the Lord what good it did her friends to pray for them all the time while she saw in them no improvement as a result of her prayers. The Lord instructed her by this comparison: "When a little child is brought back from the presence of an emperor who has enriched him with vast possessions and in immense revenue, which of those who look at his childish form can see any effect of what he has been given, athugh his future wealth and greatness are no secret from those who were witnesses? Do not be surprised, therefore, that you see no material result from your prayers, for I, in my eternal wisdom, will dispose of them in the most useful and erfect way. And no faithful prayer is without fruit, although the way in which it bears fruit is hidden from humankind."

Desiring to know what fruit there was in directing her thoughts to God, she was enlightened: When a man meditates or simply turns his attention to God, it is as though he were standing before the throne of glory holding up to God a mirror of marvelous uster, in which the Lord rejoices to see his own image reflected, because it is he who sends and directs all good things. As through his own limitations a man sometimes has difficulty in doing this, the harder he strives to do it, the more delectably does the mirror seem to shine before the face of the ever adorable Trinity and all the saints. And this will be for the abiding glory of God ad for the everlasting bliss of the soul.

One feast day when she was prevented from singing by a bad headache, she asked the Lord why he so often let this happen to her on a feast day. She received this reply: "Lest perchance you are carried away by the pleasure of singing the sacred melody and become less receptive of grace." And she said, "Your grace, Lord, can protect me from that." He rejoined: But it is easier for a person to be perfect if an occasion of falling into sin is taken away from him by his being brought low by some affliction or trouble. This brings him a twofold growth in merit, for he increases in both patience and humility."

Carried away by her love, she said to the Lord one day: "How I wish, O Lord, that my soul might burn with such a fire that it might melt and be like some liquid substance, so that it could be entirely poured out into you!" He answered: "Your will is to you such a fire." By these words she saw that it is by His will that a man receives the full effect of all the desires he has as regards God.

She had often sought by prayer to obtain from the Lord the rooting out of vices in herself and others; and had often felt that one could not do better than to ask God in His mercy to loosen the bonds which come from bad habit, so that it would be as easy to resist a vice as if the difficulty were not increased by the force of habit which we call second nature. Now she came to recognize in this the admirable plan of divine love for the salvation of humankind, which, for the increase of our eternal glory, permits us to be attacked by many and violent temptations to evil, so that we may be able to gain a more glorious victory over them.

During a sermon she heard the preacher say that no one could be saved without the love of God, and that everyone must have at least enough to be brought to repent and to abstain from sin for the sake of the love of God. She considered in her heart that, in departing this ife, more people seem to repent through a fear of hell rather than for a love of God. To this the Lord made answer: "When I see the death agony of those who have at any time found my remembrance sweet, or who have done some meritorious work, even if on the point of death, I show myself to them so full of kindness, love and mercy that they repent from the bottom of their hearts for having ever offended me, and through this repentance they are saved. And so I would like my chosen ones to praise me for this benefit, among the general benefits for which they give me thanks."

Sometimes when meditating she began to see her interior deformities and to be so displeased with herself that with anxiety she would wonder how she could ever be pleasing to God, who would see so many stains in her, for where she saw only one stain, the all-penetrating eyes of the divinity would see an infinite number. She was reassured about this by the divine reply: "Love makes pleasing." By this she understood that if on earth human love has such power that sometimes it makes the deformed pleasing for love's sake, to those who love them, and even at times so pleasing that the lovers, through the power of love, want to resemble their loved ones, how then be distrustful of God, who is Love itself? Cannot he, through the power of love, make pleasing those whom he loves?

When she was bemoaning in her heart that she could not desire to praise God as much as she should have done, she was diviney taught that God is best satisfied when we are not able to do more than want to have this great desire; our desires are great before God in proportion to our desire that they should be great. And when the heart has this desire—that is, the will to have the desire—God takes more delight in dwelling in the soul than a person could have in dwelling among flowers of springtime loveliness.

As a feast day was approaching, she began to fee unwell and she desired that the Lord might keep her well until after the feast, or at least mitigate the infirmity, that she might not be prevented from celebrating the feast; she would, however, submit herself entirely to the divine will. She received this answer from the Lord: "By asking for this, and above all because you submit your will to mine, you lead me into a little garden of delights, planted with flowers and very lovely in my sight. But, you know, then I shall be following you to the part of the garden which you yourself prefer. While, if I do not grant your prayer, and you persevere in patience, then you will be following me to the part of the garden which I like better, because I take more pleasure in you if you have this desire in spite of your trouble than if you had devotion together with sensible pleasure."

She was considering the judgment of God in giving some souls great consolation in his service, while other souls remain in a state of aridity, and was enlightened thus by God: "The heart has been created by God to hold delight, just as a vessel for holding water. Now if the vessel will gradually empty and become dry; so if the human heart that is filled with spiritual delight lets it seep out through the senses of the body, be seeing and hearing, or by allowing any of the other bodily senses to be freely indulged, it could leak out in such a way that the heart would become wholly emptied of delight in God. And anyone can experience this for himself. If one desires to see something, or to say some word in which there is little or no profit, and one does it at once, one thinks it is of no importance because it slips away as easily as water. But if one proposes to restrain oneself for God's sake, the spiritual delight will increase so much that soon the heart will be too small to contain it. Thus it is that when a man restrains himself in such matters, he comes to experience delight in God; and the harder he has to strive to do it, the more pleasure he will find in God, and the more fruitful will be his devotion.

Chapter 17 – The Lord's Condescension and the Sharing of Grace

It was the Sunday on which the feast of St. Lawrence fell, together with the anniversary of the dedication of the church. During the first Mass she was praying for some people who had devoutly asked for her prayers, when she saw the trunk of a green vine reaching from the throne of heaven down to the earth; by means of its spreading foliage ascent could be made from the bottom to the top. She understood this ascent to mean the faith whereby the chosen are raised up to heavenly things. She recognized several of the community in high places at the top, to the left of the throne, and the son of god standing with due reverence in the presence of his heavenly Father; it was at the time when the community would have been going to communion had they not been prevented from doing so by the interdict. She greatly desired that she as well as the others there present might be spiritually favored with the life-giving sacrament, through the divine mercy which no power can withstand. Then she saw the Lord Jesus holding in his hand a host which he seemed to plunge into the heart of God the Father; then he withdrew it, rosy red, as though it were stained red with blood. Very much at a loss, she asked herself what this might signify, since red is the symbol of suffering, and God the Father could never be marked by any trace of the red color of suffering. And while she was preoccupied with these thoughts, she failed to notice whether the desires she had expressed had been fulfilled, except that after a time she was aware that the Lord had found a peaceful resting-place in the heart and soul of those of the community whom she had recognized before in the high places. But she had no idea how this had come about.

Meanwhile, she remembered someone who had asked for her prayers just before Mass with humble devotion, and she prayed for her that the Lord might give her a share in the honor already mentioned. To this she received the following answer: "No one can make the ascent of faith I showed you who is not raised by confidence; and the one for whom you are praying is lacking in it.' She answered: "Lord, it seems to me that the want of confidence in that soul proceeds from humility, which you usually reward with more abundant grace." To which he answered: "I will come down and communicate my gifts to her and to all those who are in the valley which is humility." Then she saw the Lord descending by a sort of scarlet ladder and shortly afterward, he appeared in the middle of the altar of the church, clad in ponitifical vestments. In his hands he was holding a pyx like the one in which consecrated hosts are usually reserved. During the whole of the Mass until the Preface, he continued seated, turned toward the priest. And such a multitude of angels were present for his service that the whole of the church to the roght of the Lord, seemed to be filled with them. These angels showed the special joy they felt, enveloping with extreme affection this place in which their fellow-citizens, that is, the nuns of the community, were so continually offering their prayers to God. While to the left of the Lord, a choir of angels was standing near, but apart from them, the choir of apostles, and apart from them, a choir of martyrs, then the choir of confessors, and lastly the choir of virgins. While she was observing this wonder, she remembered that, according to the Scriptures, "Incorruption bringeth nearer to God!" (Wis 6:20), and she understood that between the Lord and the holy virgins there shone a particular ray of light-snow brilliance which united the virgins with the Lord more closely than all the other saints, seeming to caress them with the sweetest love and a wonderfully joyous intimacy. She also understood that some rays of admirable brilliance were falling directly onto some members of the community, as though there were no obstacle between them and the Lord; although she knew that in reality several soid walls separated them from the church in which she beheld the vision.

While she was making her thanksgiving to the Lord as best she could, rejoicing in the admirable benevolence of divine love, he gave her to understand that as often as anyone assists at Mass with devotion, in union with God who offers himself there in the sacrament for the salvatio of the whole world. God the father truly regards him with the same satisfaction as that with which he loks upon the sacred host that is being offered to him; so that person is like a man who comes out of the darkness into full sunlight, and is suddenly bathed in light. Then she questioned the Lord, saying: "And if one falls into sin, my Lord, does one immediately lose this blessedness? Just as one who leaves the sunlight to go back into darkness loses the lovely brightness of daylight?" The Lord answered: "No, although by sinning he doed shade himself to some extent from the light of God's clemency, yet my loving kindness always preserves in him a vestige of that blessedness unto eternal life, which increases in him each time he take care to assist with devotion at the reception of the sacraments."

One day, after having received communion, she was meditating on the care with which we should watch over the tongue, since it is the tongue more than all the other members of the body which receives the most precious mystery of Christ. She was instructed by this comparison: that anyone who does not restrain his tongue from uttering vain words, false, shameful, slanderous words and the like, and goes unrepentant to communion, receives Christ as if he were receiving a guest by pelting him on his arrival with the stones which were heaped with a heavy bar. Let anyone who read this lines ponder them with tears of deep compassion, considering how so much kindness can be met with so many injuries, and how he who came with gentleness for the salvation of humanity can be so cruelly treated by the very ones he came to save. The same could be said of any other sin.

Another day when she was to go to communion she felt herself insufficiently prepared; and when the time came she thus addressed her soul: "Behold, now the Bridegroom is calling you and how can you go to meet him when you are not adorned with the merits with which you ought to be prepared?" Then shrinking back still further in her great unworthiness, wholly mistrusting herself but placing all her hope in God alone, she said to herself: "What is the use of delaying? If I were to spend a thousand years in trying, left to myself I could still never prepare myself worthily, since I am not aboul to provide anything which would serve for the appropriate lavish preparation. Yet I shall set out to meet him with humility and faith; and when he sees me from a long way off. Moved by his own love, he is powerful enough to send to meet me everything I need in order to present myself, fittingly prepared, to him." With these despositions she went forward, keeping the eyes of her heart fixed on her deformities and disorders.

Chapter 19 – How to Pray to the Mother of God

It was the hour of prayer and, coming into the presence of God, she asked him what the subject he would most like her to apply herself in that hour. The Lord answered: "Keep close to my mother who us seated at my side and strive to praise her. Then she devoutly hailed the Queen of heaven with the verse: "Paradise of pleasure..." praising her for having been the most pleasant abode which God;s inscrutable wisdom, to whom all creatures are known, chose as his dwelling from among all the delectable pleasures of the Father. She prayed that she might obtain for her own heart such attractive and varied virtues that God might be pleased to dwell there also. At that, the blessed Virgin seemed to bend down, as though to plant in the heart of the suppliant various flowers of virtue, such as the rose of charity, the violet of humility, the hoeliotrope of obedience, and others of the same sort, showing by this how eager she always is to hear the prayers of those who call upon her.

...After a little time had passed, Gertrude said to the Lord: "O my brother, since you were made man to make up for all human defects, now deighn to make up to your blessed Mother for what may have been lacking in my praise of her When he heard these words, the son of God arose and most reverently went to kneel before his Mother, bowing his head, he saluted her most courteously and affectionately, so that she could not but be pleased with the homage of one whose imperfections were so abundantly made up for her by her most beloved Son.

The following day, as he was praying in this way, the Virgin Mother appeared to her in the presence of the every adorable Trinity, which appeared I the form of a fleur-de-lys, as it is usually shown, with three petals, one erect and two durning downward. Thus she was given to understand that the Blessed Mother of God is judtly called the White Lily of the Trinity, because she has received into herself, more fully and perfectly than any other creature, the virtues of the adorable Trinity; virtues which she never stained with even the least speck of venial sin.

The erect petal denotes the omnipotence of God the Father; the two turning downward, the Wisdom and Love of the Son and the Holy Spirit, whom she most resembles. Wherefore she understood from the blessed Virgin that is one were to salute her devoutly with the words: "White Lily of the Trinity and fairest Rose of heavenly bliss," she would show how great is her power through the omnipotence of the Father; and with what ingenuity she knows how to work for the salvation of the human race, through the wisdom of the Son; and how immeasurably her heart abounds in tenderness, through the love of the Holy Spirit.

The Blessed Virgin added: "Besides this, at the hour of death, I shall appear to the soul who salutes me in this way in a blossoming of such beauty that she will be wondrously consoled as I reveal to her the bliss of heaven." From that time Gertrude resolved to salute the Blessed Virgin, or her images with these words:

"Hail, white Lily of the resplendent and ever tranquil Trinity! Fairest Rose of heaven's bliss! The King of heaven chose to be born to you, to be fed with your milk! Oh, feed our souls on the outpourings of divine grace!"

...Then she prayed for those who had commended themselves to her that the Lord might give to each of them an increase of his grace. She received this reply: "I have given to everyone a golden tube of such power that he may draw whatever he desires from the infinite depths of my divine heart." This tube she understood to mean free will, through which a man may claim for his own every spiritual good, both heavenly and earthly. For eample, if anyone ardently longs to be able to give God praise, thanksgiving, service and fidelity equal to that which any saint has ever given him, such a desire is as agreeable to the immense goodness of Gos as though it had actually been carried out. But this tube takes on its brilliant gold color when a person thanks God for having given him a will of such nobility that with it he cana gain infinitely more than the whole world could achieve with all its powers. [Ch. 30]

"...In Advent, at the responsoty "Ecce Dominus protector noster, sanctus Israel," she understood that if someone applies himself with all his heart to desire that his whole life be governed, in prosperity and adversity, according to the most laudable will of God, then by such thoughts, with God's grace, he would be giving as much honor to God as one would give to an emperor in placing the imperial crown on his head. [Ch. 30]

Once when they were singing in honor of a martyrm "Qui vult venire post me," she saw the Lord walking along a path, pleasant to behold, with fairest flowers and venrdure, but narrow and lined with dense hedges bristling with sharp thorns. She saw that he seemed to be preceded by a cross which parted the thorns and made the way wider and easier. With a serene expression on his face, turning toward those who belonged to him, he invited them to follow him, saying: "Whoever wishes to come after me, let him deny himself, and take up his cross and follow me." From this, she knew that the cross of each is his own personal trial. For example, for some souls obedience is a cross, when they are obliged to do what is contrary to their wishes; for others, to be burdened with infirmity, which acts as a restraint; and so on. We should all carry our crosses and apply ourselves with a good will to suffer adversity gladly, and in addition to do all that is in our power, neglecting nothing which we know to be for the greater glory of God." [Ch. 30]

"Again, on the feast of several martyrs while they were singing 'The glorious blood...' she realized that although blood is in itself an unpleaant thing, it is praised in Scripture because it is shed for Christ; similarly, the neglect of religious duties, for motives of obedience or fraternal charity, please God so much that it too might well be termed glorious.

On another occasion she understood how God, by a hidde dispensation of his judgment, sometimes permits wicked people, when they try to tempt chosen souls by deceitfully asking them to disclose secrets, to receive a reply which on;y serves to make them persist in obstinacy and error. And this is to the detriment of the wicked, but to the advantage of the just. That is why we find in Ezekiel: "If anyone place his uncleanness in his heart and set up a stumbling block of his iniquity before his face and shall come to the prophet inquiring of me by him, I the Lord will answer him according to the multitude of his uncleanness; that he may be caught in his own heart..." (Ez 14:4-5).

By the versicle, 'Vouchsafe, O Lord this day," she understood that whenever a man commends himself to God, praying that he will keep him from sin, then, even if it seems to that man, by the hidden designs of God, that he has fallen into some grave sin, yet he will never sin in such a way that he lacks the grace of God, which will support him like a staff and lead him easily to repentance.

While they were singing the Responsory, "Benedicens..." she presented herself to the Lord as though she were Noah in person, imploring him to give her his blessing. After this was done, the Lord himself in his turn seemed to be asking her for a blessing. Then she understood that a man is blessing God when he says in his heart that he repents of having offended his creator and implores his help to prevent him from falling again into sin. At this blessing the Lord of heaven bowed low, showing her that this was as acceptable to him as though that blessing had been responsible for all his beatitude.

Again, by these words, "Where is thy brother Abel?" she comprehended that God requires every religious to give an account of whatever is done against the Rule by his fellow religious. If such a fault could have been prevented in some way, either by personal admonition or by reporting to the superior. The excuse which some people give, "It is not my duty to correct my brother," or "I am worse than he is," will be no better received by God than were the words of Cain; "Am I my brother's keeper?" (Gen 4:9). Everyone who is held repsonsible before God for restraining his brother from evil and encouraging him to do good. And each time that he fails in this, against his conscience, he sins against God. And it is in vain that he claims that he did not receive the charge to do so, because the charge is truly from God, as his conscience tells him. If he neglects this duty, God will require an account of it from his soul, and perhaps more from his soul than from the soul of the superior, who was either not present or, if he was, perhaps did not notice. Wherefore there are the menacing words of Scripture: 'Woe to those who do evil; wor to those who consent (Rom 1:32). He who consents to evil practices deceit in concealing it when, by disclosing it, he could show forth God's praise.

From the Responsory "Induit me Dominus," she understood that anyone who works in words or deeds, to promote the cause of religion, and who fights in the lawful cause of justice, clothes the Lord, so to speak, in a rich garment of honor and glory. And the Lord will reward him in eternal life according to the riches of his royal liberality, clothing him with joy as with a garment and, as an additional reward, he will deck his brow with a crown of spiritual glory (Is 61:10). But in particular she understood that if in advancing the cause of good or of religion one suffers adversity, it is more acceptable to God, just as a garment is more acceptable to a pauper if it warms as well as clothes him. And if someone who tries to promote the cause of religion is prevented by others from having any success his merit is not in the least diminished in God's sight.

While they were singing the Responsory, "Vocavit angelus Domini," she realized how hosts of angels surround the elect and are fully sufficient to protect them. But if the Lord in his fatherly providence sometimes suspends this protection and lets his chosen ones be tried in some way, it is in order that they may be the more gloriously rewarded; their reward will be allthe greater if they have triumphed by their own virtue while the custody and protection of their guardian angels have, so to say, been withheld.

Again, as a consequence of that Responsory, she understood that, just as holy Abraham stretched forth his arm in obedience and so deserved to be called by an angel, so the elect, when he bends his mind wholeheartedly to do some difficult work for God, is instantly smiled on by the sweetness of divine grace and deservedly consoled by his own conscience. And so in the boundless liberality of God he is given this consolation even before his eternal reward; for each will receive a reward appropriate to his labor.

Once, when she was reflecting on the adversities of her past life, she asked the Lord why he had allowed her to be troubled by certain persons. To that she received the following reply: "When a fatherly hand is raised to chastise the child, the rod cannot resist. And so I could wish that my chosen ones would never blame the persons by whom they are tried, but should always consider that, in my fatherly affection, I would never let the faintest breath of wind blow against them if I were not looking to the eternal salvation they will receive as their reward; rather let them have compassion on those who stain their own souls for their purification."

One day she was having difficulty with a certain task, and she said to God the Father: "Lord, I offer you this work through your only Son, in the power of the Holy Spirit, to your eternal praise." She knew the power of these words to be such that in a marvelous way they elevate any work done with that intention far beyond human estimation, so that whatever is offered is made pleasing to God the Father. Just as that which is seen through a green glass appears to be green, or red, if seen through a red glass, and so on, whatever is offered to God the Father through his only-begotten Son becomes most pleasing and acceptable to him.

Once as she was praying she asked the Lord what good it did her friends to pray for them all the time, while she was in them no improvement as a result of her prayers. The Lord instructed her by this comparison: "When a little child is brought bak from the presence of an emperor who has enriched him with vast possessions and an immense revenue, which of those who look at his childish form can see any effect of what he has been given, although his future wealth and greatness are no secret from those who were witnesses? Do not be surprised, therefore, that you see no material result from your prayers, for I, in my eternal wisdom, will dispose of them in the most useful and perfect way. And no faithful prayer is without fruit, although the way in which it bears fruit is hidden from humankind."

During a sermon she heard the preacher say that no one could be saved without the love of God, and that everyone must have at least enough to be brought to repent and to abstain from sin for the sake of the love of God. She considered in her heart that, in departing this life, more people seem to repent through a fear of hell rather than for love of God. To this the Lord made answer: "When I see the death agony of those who have at any time found my remembrance sweet, or who have done some meritorious work, even if on the point of death, I show myself to them so full of kindness, love and mercy that they repent from the bottom of their hearts for having ever offended me, and through this repentance they are saved. And so I would like my chosen ones to praise me for this benefit, among the general benefits for which they give me thanks."

Sometimes when meditating she began to see her interior deformities and to be so displeased with herself that with anxiety she would wonder how she could ever be pleasing to God, who would see so many stains in her, for where she saw only one stain, the all-penetrating eyes of the divinity would see an infinite number. She was reassured about this by the divine reply: "Love makes pleasing." By this she understood that if on earth human love ha such power that sometimes it makes the deformed pleasing, for love's sake, to those who love them, and even at times so pleasing that the lovers, through the power of love, want to resemble, their loved ones, how then be distrustful of God, who is Love itself? Cannot he, through the power of love, make pleasing those whom he loves.

One day she was reflecting on the numerous and wonderful graces she had received so freely from God's love, deeming herself to be most wretched and unworthy of every good things, since she had accepted such innumerable gifts from God and had wasted them so carelessly that they seemed to have borne no fruits—for neither had they increased her enjoyment or her thanksgiving, nor had they helped others, to whom, had they been made known, they might have tended to some edification or been a means of bringing them to know God better. She was consoled by being enlightened thus on the subject; The Lord does not bestow his gifts of grace on his chosen ones in order to exact from each a worthy fruit, for he knows that human frailty often prevents that. But the overflowing love and generosity of God cannot restrain itself; although he knows a man is not able to make use of all of them, he assiduously pours forth a great quantity of extra graces, in order that the man may at least receive a great quantity of blessedness in the future. It is just like this with the earthly things which are sometimes given to a child who has, at the time, no idea of the use they will be to him; when he is grown up, he will derive much profit from them. Similarly, the Lord, in giving graces to his elect in this life, is preparing them and making them suited to the things in whose enjoyment will consist their eternal beatitude in heaven.

When she was bemoaning in her heart that she sould not desire to please God as much as she should have done, she was divinely taught that God is best satisfied when we are not able to do more than want to have this great desire; our desires are great before God in proportion to our desire that they should be great. And when the heart has this dwelling in the soul than a person could have in dwelling among flowers of springtime loveliness.

On another occasion she was prevented by bodily infirmity from giving her attention fully to God for some days; when she came to herself, her conscience was troubled. With devout humility she set herself to confess her fault to the Lord.

And although she feared she would have to toil for a long time to regain the sweetness of divine grace, suddenly, in an instant, she felt the gentle kindness of God, who was bending over her with the tenderest embrace, and saying: "Daughter, you are always with me and all I have is yours" (Lk 15:31). These neglect to direct our attention to God, his loving mercy never fails to consider all our works to be worthy of an eternal reward, so long as the will does not turn away from God, and one makes frequent acts of contrition for everything for which the conscience feels remorse.

She was considering the judgment of God in giving some souls great consolation in his service, while other souls remain in a state of aridity, and was enlightened thus by God: "The heart has been created by God to hold delight, just as a vessel for holding water. Now if the vessel holding water lets it seep out through any small cracks, the vessel will gradually empty and become dry; so if the human heart that is filled with spiritual delight lets it seep out through the senses of the body, by seeing and hearing, or by allowing any of the other bodily senses to be freely indulged, it could leak out in such a way that the heart would become wholly emptied of delight in God. And anyone can experience this for himself. If one desires to see something, or to say some word in which there is little or no profit, and one does it at once, one thinks it is of no importance, because it slips away as easily as water. But if one proposes to restrain oneself for God's sake, the spiritual delight will increase so much that soon the heart will be too small to contain it. Thus it is that when a man restrains himself in such matters, he comes to experience delight in God; and the harder he has to strive to do it, the more pleasure he will find in God, and the more fruitful will be his devotion.

On another occasion she was feeling worn out and said to the Lord: "O my Lord, what is to become of me? What do you want of me?" The Lord answered: "As a mother comforts her child, I will comfort you. Haven't you ever seen a mother caressing her child?" At this, she was silent, not being able to remember. The Lord recalled to her mind that scarcely six months before she had seen a mother fondling her little child, and he reminded her especially of three things which she had not noticed at th time. First, the mother often asked her little child to kiss her, at which the little one was obliged to riase himself with an effort on his little weak legs. The Lord added that it was necessary to raise oneself with a great effort by means of contemplation to the enjoyment of the sweetness of his love. Second, the mother tested the will of her child, saying: "Do you want this? Do you want this or that?" and let him have nothing . So God tries a man when he makes him foresee great troubles which never come to anything. However, when a man submits willingly, God is fully satisfied and makes him worthy of an eternal reward. Third, when the child spoke, no one present could understand a word the little boy said, save only his mother. So only God can understand man's intention and judges him accordingly, far otherwise than man, who sees only exterior things.

Asking the Lord what he would like her to apply her thoughts to at that time, she received this reply from him, "i want you to learn patience." It chanced that just then she was very much upset about something. She said to him: "And how and by what means can I learn this?" Then the Lord, lifting her up like a kind teacher who holds his little pupil close to his breast, proposed to her three ways of acquiring patience, as if he were teaching her three letters, saying in the first place: "Consider hos great is the affectionate intimacy with which a king addresses the person who above all others is most like him in every way; judge, therefore, how my affection for you grows when you suffer with patience for my sake contempt like that which I suffered." In the second place, he aid: "Again, consider with what respect the friend of a king, who resembles him in everything, is treated by all his subjects; and judge what glory your patience is laying up for you in the court of heaven." Then in the third place, he said: "Consider what comfort can be given by the consoling caresses of a faithful friend; judge, therefore with what sweet tenderness I shall console you in heaven for the least of the things which afflict your mind here."

During the Mass for the Dead, while they were singing the Tract, "Sicut cervus," at the words, "My soul thirsts," trying to rouse herself from her tepidity, she said to the Lord: "Alas, my Lord, how lukewarm re my desires for you, my true good, since I can so seldom truly say to you that my soul thirsts for you." The Lord replied: "Say to me not seldom, but very often that your soul thirsts for me; for the merciful love with which I desire man's salvation compels me to believe that whenever my chosen ones desire some good thing, it is really myself they desire, since all good things are in me and come from me. For example, if a man desires health, ease, wisdom, and the like, in order to increase his merit I often consider that it is myself that he desires unless he deliberately turns away from me, that is, if he desires to have wisdom that he may boast f it, or health that he may do amiss. And for that reason I frequently afflict those who are specially dear to me with infirmities of the body or distress of the mind and so on, so that when they desire the good which is the opposite of these ills, the ardent love of my heart causes me to reward them more abundantly, with the generosity which is my delight. [Ch 32].

On another occasion something similar was made known to her by divine inspiration; that is, the Lord, who delights to be with the children of men (Prov. 8:31)--although he may find in men nothing that could make them sufficiently pleasing to be worthy of his presence—sometimes sends them troubles or sorrows, either of body or of spirit, precisely in order to have the opportunity to stay with them, as the Scriptures truly say: "The Lord is nigh unto them that are of a contrite heart (Ps. 33:19). And again: "I am with him in tribulation" (Ps. 90:15).

When we consider this and similar things, we are forced to cry out from the depths of our hearts with all the gratitude and love of which our human frailty is capable, the words of the Apostle: "Oh, the depths of the riches of the wisdom and of the knowledge of God! How incomprehensible are his judgments, and how unsearchable his ways!" (Rom. 11:33). How inventive he is in working for the salvation of humankind!

One night she had fallen asleep when the Lord visited her in a dream so sweetly that she seemed to be as much refreshed by the intimate fellowship of the Lord's presence as by the most delicious banquet. On awaking she said to him in gratitude: "How is it, Lord God, that I, most unworthy should receive this, rather than others who are often so much troubled in dreams that their cri terrify those who hear them?" He answered: "If those whom my fatherly providence disposes to sanctify through suffering seek, while they are awake, to procure comfort for their bodies and so deprive themselves of occasions of merit then, in my divine love, I trouble them with dreams which I send them so that they may merit at least something." She asked, "But Lord, how can they acquire merit if they have no intention of suffering and do so, as it were, against their will?" He explained: "My goodness accomplishes this. In the world, those who wear ornaments of glass or copper do indeed appear to be adorned, but those who wear gold and real gems must be considered to be very much wealthier, the same applies in this case."

Once, when she was reciting the Canonical Hours with less attention than usual she saw at her side the anient enemy of humankind, who, in mocking guise, recited the rest of the psalm "thy testimonies are wonderful..." (Ps. 118:129), hastily slurring over and suppressing words and syllables. When he had finished, he said: "Well, has your creator, your savior and your lover, employe his gifts in giving you such facility of speech! You can make eloquent discourses on any subject whenever you want, but when you speak to him your words are so hasty and careless that just now in this psalm you left out this number of letters, this number of syllables, and this nummber of words." Then she ralized that if this wily enemy had caounted so exactly the letters and syllables, it was so that after death he could bring grave accusations against those who tend to say the Hours of the Divine Office in a hurry and without real attention.

When she came to Mass, very weak and longing for spiritual communion, it happened that the priest who had taken the body of Christ to a sick person was returning from the village. At the sound of the bell, she was filled with desire and said to the Lord: "Oh, how gladly would I receive you now, life of my soul, at least spiritually had I but a little time in which to prepare myself!" He replied: "The eyes of my divine love will prepare you most fittingly. Upon which she saw the Lord looking at her, directing rays of sunlight into her soul and saying, "I will fix my eyes upon thee" (Ps. 31:8). By these words she understood that three things were effected in the soul by the divine gaze, which was like the sun, and that there were three ways in which the soul should prepare to receive them. First, the ook of divine love, like the sun, takes away all stains from the soul, purifying it and making it whiter than snow (Ps. 50:9). And this effect can be gained by the humble recognition of one's own defects. Second, the look of divine love melts the soul and fits it to receive spiritual gifts, just as wax is melted by the sun's heat and made ready to take the imprint of a seal. And this effect the soul obtains by devout intentions. Third, the look of divine love makes the soul fruitful, so as to bring forth and multiply its various fruits. And this effect is obtained by faithful trust; for if a person abandons hiself wholly to God, faithfully trusting in God's boundless love, everything, whether in adversity or in prosperity, will work together unto good (Rom. 8:28). [Ch. 39].

Chapter 40 – How the Son of God Appeases God the Father

On another occasion she was trying to choose from among all the gifts which the Lord in his generous love had graciously bestowed on her the one which would be most useful to show to other people for the sake of their progress. The Lord, entering into her thoughts and desires, gave her this answer: "It is very profitable for people to remember this: That I, the Son of the virgin, stand before God the Father to intercede for the salvation of the human race. And whenever, through human frailty they fall into some sin in their hearts, I offer my immaculate heart to God the Father for their amendment; when they sin with their lips, I offer my most innocent lips; when they sin with their hands, I show my pierced hands. And so on in a similar way, whatever their sin may be, at once my innocence appeases God the Father, so that penitents may always easily obtain forgiveness. And so I would like my chosen ones, whenever they have prayed for the forgiveness of their faults, always to give me thanks for having obtained for them that this should be so easily granted.

One Friday as evening was falling, she was looking at a crucifix. Moved to compunction she said to the Lord: "Ah, my sweetest Lover, how many and how cruel sufferings you endured this day for my salvation, and I, alas, in my infidelity have made so little of it that I have passed the day occupied with other matters; I have not spent this day calling to mind with devotion what you, my eternal salvation, suffered for me at each hour, and that you, who are life itself and give life to all things, died for love of me!"

The Lord replied to her from the cross: "That which you were neglecting, I myself have supplied for you. For instance, every hour I gathered into my heart what you should have been recollecting in your heart, ad afterward my heart was exceeedingly full. Almost bursting with great desire, I have longed for this hour when you would make this intention your own. Now, with that intention of yours, I want to offer to God my Father all that which I have supplied for you throughout this day, for without your intention my action could not be so conducive to your salvation.

In this can be seen how very faithful is the love of God for humankind. In return for this single intention, whereby a man recognized and is sorry for what he has neglected, the Lord makes amends to God the Father and supplies fully, in the highest degree, for every defect, for which it is right that everyone should praise him.

Again, as she was holding a crucifix in her hand with devout attention, she was given to understand that if anyone were to look with a similar devout attention at an image of Christ crucified, the Lord would look at them with such benign mercy that their soul, like a burnished mirror would reflect, by an effect of divine love, such a delectable image, that it would gladden the whole court of heaven. And as often as anyone does this on earth with affection and due devotion, it will be to his eternal glory in the future.

Another time she received this instruction: That when a person turns toward a crucifix, he is to consider in his heart that the Lord Jesus is saying to him in gentle tones: "See how I hung upon the cross for love of you, naked and despised, my body covered with wounds and every limb pulled out of joint. And now my heart is moved with such sweet charity you that, if if were expedient for your salvation, and if you could be saved in no other way, I would bear for you alone all that you may imagine I bore for the whole world." By such meditations the heart of man is incited to gratitude, because truly one cannot look at a crucifix without being touched by God's grace. Therefore a Christian so lacking in gratitude as to underestimate the immense price of his salvation could not be considered blameless; for never can one look devoutly upon a crucifix without receiving some fruit.

On another occasion, when she was occupied in thinking about the Lord's passion, she understood that meditations on the prayers or passages of Scripture which deal with the Lord's passion are infinitely more efficacious than any others. As it is impossible to touch flour without getting dusty, so no one can think about the Lord's passion with any devotion and not derive some fruit from it. Indeed, even if one only reads something about the passion, one is preparing one's soul to receive at least some of its fruits; for the intention of a person who calls to mind the passion of Christ bears more fruit than the many intentions of another who pays no heed to the Lord's passion. Let us try, therefore, to turn over in our minds more frequently the subject of Christ's passion, so that it may be for us honey in the mouth, music in the ear, gladness in the heart.

...Then she began to desire that the Lord would restore her former health, so that she might observe the Rule of her Order with greater exactitude and fervor. To which the kind Lord replied: "And why should my spouse seek to displease me by opposing my will?" She asked: "But does this desire of mine seem to you to be contrary to your will, since it seems to me that in it I do nut seek your glory?" The Lord replied: "These words of yours are but childish babblings, and so I shall not pay any attention to them, but if you go on insisting more importunately, I shall not be pleased."

She understood by these words that if one desires good health in order to serve God, one does well; but that it is more perfect by far to commit oneself entirely to the divine will, trusting that God ordains for each one whatever is best for him and his salvation, whether it be prosperity or adversity. [Ch. 44].

When she saw the others assembling for the sermon, she complained within herself and said to the Lord: "You know, my dearest, how gladly I would now hear the sermon with all my heart, were I not held back by sickness." To which the Lord answered: "Would you like me to preach to you, my dearest?" Then the Lord made her lean against his heart, with the heart of her soul close to his divine heart. When her soul had sweetly rested there a while, she heard in the Lord's heart two wondrous and very sweet pulsations.

The Lord said to her: "Each of these two pulsations brings about mans salvation in three ways. The first pulsation effects the salvation of sinners; the second, that of the just. With the first pulsation, first, I address God the Father, ceaselessly appeasing him and leading him to have mercy upon sinners. Second, I invoke all my saints, excusing the sinner with fraternal fidelity, and urging them to pray for him. Third, I address the sinner himself, calling upon him to rpent, and awaiting his conversion with ineffable longing.

With the second pulsation, first, I address God the Father, inviting him to rejoice with me for having shed my precious blood to such a good purpose for the redemption of the just, in whose hearts I now find so many delights. Second, I address all the heavenly hosts, inviting them to praise the lives of the just, and to thank me for the benefits I have already bestowed upon them, and for those I will bestow in the future. Third, I address the just themselves, lavishing various favors on them for their salvation and admonishing them to progress from day to day and from hour to hour. And just as the pulsations of the human heart are not impeded by seeing or hearing or by any manual work, but always maintain their regular motion, so the government and disposition of heaven and earth and the whole universe can never affect in the very least these twofold pulsations of my divine heart, still them, modify them, or in any way hinder them, till the end of time.

Chapter 60 – Renewal of the Sacraments

One day she was examining her conscience and found there something she would like to have confessed. As she could not have recourse to a confessor, following her usual custom she took refuge with her only solace, the Lord Jesus Christ and bewailed her difficulty. To which he responded I these words: "Why are you troubled, my love?" As often as you ask it of me, I, who am myself High Priest and true Pontiff (Heb 3:1), I shall be ready to renew in your soul all seven sacraments at once, more effectively than any priest or bishop could be one at a time. I will baptize you with my precious blood; I will confirm you in the strength of my victory.; I will espouse you to me in my faithful love (Hos 2:20): I will consecrate you in the perfection of my most holy life, in my loving mercy I will absolve you from the bonds of every sin, in my overflowing charity. I will feed you with myself, and will be refreshed by you. And the sweetness of my spirit and penetrate your whole being with such beneficent unction that through every sense and movement devotion will be, so to speak, distilled and so, without ceasing, you will be ever more prepared and sanctified for eternal life."

Chapter 61 – The Effect of Charity

Another time, although still very weak, she had got up for Matins. She had just finished one Nocturn when she was joined by another sick person with whom she had the charity to recommence Matins, not without great fatigue. During Mass, when she was praying still more devoutly to the Lord,, it seemed to her that she saw her soul very marvelously adorned with precious jewels and shining with a wonderful brightness. Divinely instructed,, she understood that she had merited this adornment because she had humbly and charitably recited again with the younger nun that part of Matins which she had recited before, and that the shining ornaments were equal in number to the words she has thus repeated. Then she remembered some negligences which she had not yet confessed, being prevented from doing so by the absence of a confessor, and bewailed this to the Lord. He answered: "Why are you complaining of your negligence, seeing that the robe of charity, which covers a multitude of sins, so gloriously envelops you?" (I Pet. 4:8). She said: "How can I be consoled by the fact that charity covers my faults, when I know that I am stained by so many of them?" to this he replied: "Charity not only covers sins, but by its warmth, which acts like that of the sun, it consumes and utterly destroys all the negligences of venial sins and even confers extra merit."

...At this, when she considered the sublimity of divine love in all that concerned her salvation, in her profound gratitude, she broke forth into devout praises. Then she saw that the ornaments she had been given for her tribulation, which looked like flowers and were very light in weight although brilliant, took on a ertain weight when, in her gratitude, she sang praises to God for her adversity. And from this she understood that the grace which God gives to make us able to praise him in adversity compensates in a nobler way for what is wanting in the weight of our affliction, just as an ornament of pure gold is more precious than a silver ornament gilded only on the surface.

Then she said: "Alas, God of my heart (Ps. 72:26), why do you put into my head so many different desires which are never to be fulfilled? Only a few days ago you put into my head the thought of hastening the reception of the sacrament of extreme unction and kindled my desire for it. WhileI was occupied with various thoughts about this, you filled me with joy and gave me many consolations concerning it. And now, on the contrary, you provoke me to desire to go away to a new religious foundation in another place, when I am so weak that I could hardly walk as far as would be required."

The Lord replied, "According to what I have already said at the beginning of the book, I have planned to give you to be a light to the Gentiles (Is. 42:6; 49:6), that is, to anlighten many souls. It is necessary that in your book everyone should find instruction and consolation, each according to his capacity. Besides, friends often enjoy talking together about many things which will never come to pass. And sometimes, too, a friend will propose to another some difficult project, so that he may have a certain proof of his friend's fidelity and, more particularly, of the generosity of his good will toward himself. I, too, delight in proposing to my chosen ones many difficult projects which will never come about, in order to have proof of their love for me and their fidelity, so that I may reward them afterwar for these great things which they will in fact never have the opportunity of doing, because I look upon their good will alone as though it were the accomplishment of their good intentions. And so, in a way, it was I who suggested to you a desire for death and so for hastening the reception of the sacrament of extreme unction. So all the devout and earnest preparations which you made then, both interiorly and exteriorly, I have already laid up for you in the secret depths of my heart, in view of your eternal salvation. You are therefore to know that, as it is said, 'But the just man, if he be prevented with death, shall be in rest' (Wis. 4:7), if by sudden death, or to receive the sacrament of extreme unction after losing consciousness (as often happens with very great saints), you would come to no harm thereby. For all the things you have done for so many years past to prepare yourself for death shall grow green again ad produce fruits for your eternal salvation, in union with the power of my divine action."

Chapter 65 – The Efforts Required to Obtain Benefits

At the request of a certin person Gertrude was offering to the Lord all the things which, through the free gift of his love, he had deigned to do in her, and was asking him to grant a share to this person. Suddenly, this person for whom she was praying appeared to her I the presesnce of the Lord who, seated on a glorious throne, was holding on his knees a robe, marvelously embroidered, which he was presenting to this person without, as yet, clothing her in it. In astonishment Gertrude said to the Lord: "When a few days ago I made you a similar offering for the soul of a poor deceased person for whom I was then praying, you deigned to raise her withut delay to the supreme joys of heaven. Why, kindest Lord, through the merits of these same graces which you have accorded to me, most unworthy, do you not clothe this person, who so much desires it, with the robe you are presenting to her?" He answered: "When I am offered something in charity for the souls of the faithful departed then, out of the love which is natural to me (for it is in my nature always to be merciful and to spare), since I know that they can no longer help themselves in any way. I take pity on their misery and immediately grant to them whatever has been offered for them, in absolution of sins or in alleviation of their sufferings, or to increase their eternal felicity, according to the state and merit of each. But when a similar offering is made for the living, certainly I use it for their salvation, but since they themselves may still work for their own salvation by good works, good desires, and good will, it is but fitting that what they wish to obtain through the merits of others, they should try to merit through their own labors. That is why, if the person for whom you are praying wishes to be clothed with the benefits which I have bestowed upon you, she should try to apply herself spiritually to three things: first, let her bow down in humility and gratitude to receive the robe, that is, let her confess humbly to needing the merits of others and give me heartfelt thanks for being willing to mae good her poverty through the riches of others. Second, let her take this robe with hope and trust, that is, hoping in my goodness and trusting that great profit will come of it for the progress of her soul. Third, let her put on this robe by exercising herself in charity and in other virtues. And let all who desire to have a share in the blessings and merits of others do likewise; in this way they will be able to receive profit from them."

To order more books by Dusty Rose go to Amazon/Kindle:

ROSE Book of Saints

Catechism of St. Teresa of Avila

The ABC's of the Catholic Faith

Printed in Great Britain
by Amazon